CONTENTS

WORLD OF MACHINES

It's hard to imagine a world without machines. We rely on them for many things, from cooking meals and moving about to keeping in touch with other people. A machine is a device that contains several parts and is designed to do a particular job. The first machines were 'mechanical', meaning that they worked with moving parts. Today, we still use mechanical machines, but we also have others that work with sound, light or electricity. In this book, you can find out how different parts work to make a machine work.

Gears

Gears are toothed wheels that fit together so that they turn each other around. Gears are important parts of many machines, because they can change the direction and force of a movement. The change depends on the relative sizes of the 2 gears. You can find out more about gears on pages 16-17.

Levers

A lever is something rigid that can pivot around a point (fulcrum). Levers can also change the direction and force of a movement. For more on levers, see pages 8-9.

Screw

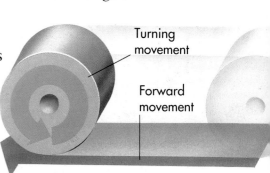

Spiral thread

Screw thread

A screw moves into wood with a great forward force, thanks to its gently sloping thread. Many machines use screw threads to increase a force in this way. As you can see on pages 8-9 they make work easier, but they also make it last longer.

Small gear turns twice as far, but with half the force

Fulcrum

Wheels

Many machines have parts that turn around. On pages 12-13 you can see how wheels move things about. On pages 14-15 you can learn what happens when they move fast.

Turning movement

Forward movement

Heating and cooling

If you go for a run, or take some other kind of exercise, your body will warm up. In the same way, machines make heat when they work. As you can find out on pages 24-25 some machines are designed specially to make heat. They do this by burning a fuel or by using electricity, and they pass on the heat to a place where it is needed. Cooling machines are designed to do exactly the opposite. On pages 26-27 you can see how they help heat to flow from one place to another.

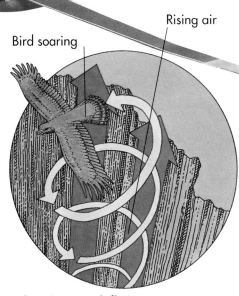

Bird soaring

Rising air

Floating and flying

Floating and flying are 2 ways of moving through a fluid (liquid or gas). On pages 28-31 you can find out what keeps a balloon or a bird in the air, and how a helicopter manages to take off vertically, or even fly backwards.

Using sound and light

Sound and light are 2 different forms of energy. Sound travels through matter, but light can even travel through empty space. On pages 36-39 you can find out about machines that give out sound and light, and about ones that take it in, so that it can be stored or converted into something else.

Eyepiece

Target plate

Cassette

Lens

Computers

Computers are the fastest-changing machines today. They work by converting information into pulses of electricity. On pages 42-43 you can find out more about these pulses.

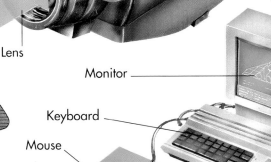

Monitor

Keyboard

Mouse

Computer

MAKING THINGS MOVE

Whenever you move anything, or change its shape, you have to exert a force. You do this by using your muscles. Machines with moving parts work in a similar way, producing forces by harnessing several different sources of energy. Some machines get their energy from things that are already moving, such as air or water. Others obtain energy by releasing it from a fuel, or by harnessing electricity. Once something has started to move, it needs a steady supply of energy to keep it going.

FORCE OF WIND

Getting going
To make a skateboard move, you have to exert a force with one of your legs. But you don't push your leg in the direction that you want to go. Instead, you push backwards. This creates a force

Forward force of reaction

Backward force exerted by leg

called reaction which moves the skateboard forwards. Reaction appears whenever a force is exerted, and it always pushes in the opposite direction.

Inertia and momentum
It's easy to stop a light moving object, such as a table-tennis ball. But if the ball was filled with lead, you would find stopping it a lot more difficult. This is because the lead-filled ball has a much higher 'inertia' which means that it takes much more energy to stop.
   Inertia is important in machines. It means that heavy parts are difficult to set in motion, but once they are moving, they take a long

Thrust moves board forward

time to slow down. An object's 'momentum' is a measure of how much energy of movement it has. The 2 skateboarders shown here have exactly the same momentum.

Heavy object moves a short distance

Light object moves a long distance

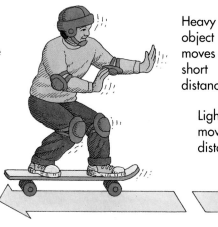

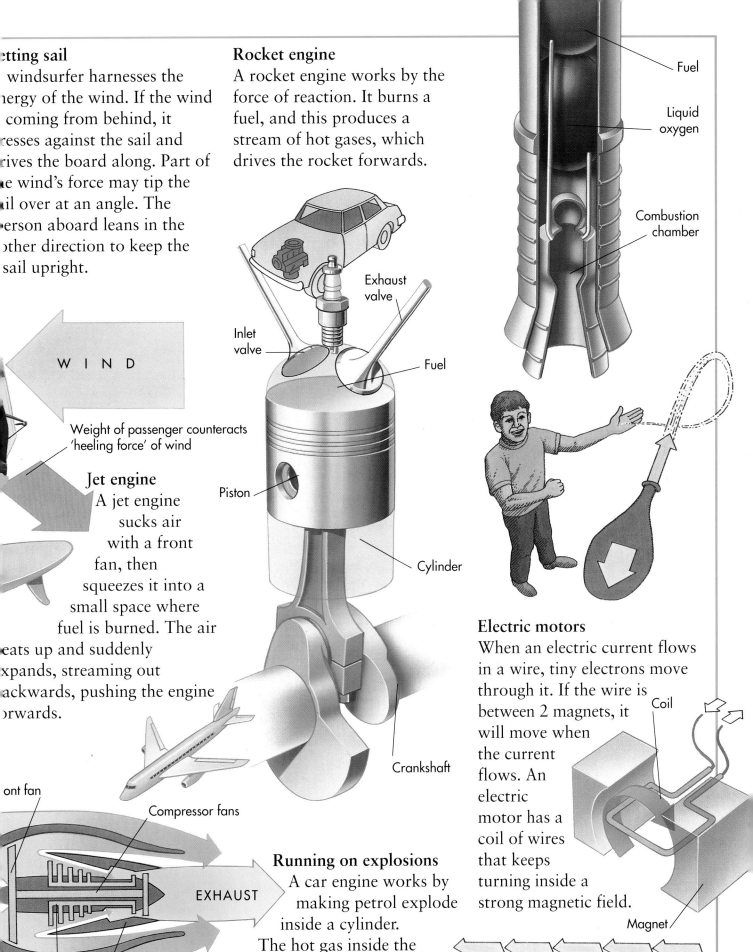

etting sail

windsurfer harnesses the nergy of the wind. If the wind coming from behind, it resses against the sail and rives the board along. Part of ne wind's force may tip the il over at an angle. The erson aboard leans in the other direction to keep the sail upright.

WIND

Weight of passenger counteracts 'heeling force' of wind

Jet engine

A jet engine sucks air with a front fan, then squeezes it into a small space where fuel is burned. The air eats up and suddenly xpands, streaming out ackwards, pushing the engine orwards.

ont fan

Compressor fans

EXHAUST

Fan shaft   Combustion chamber

Rocket engine

A rocket engine works by the force of reaction. It burns a fuel, and this produces a stream of hot gases, which drives the rocket forwards.

Exhaust valve

Inlet valve

Fuel

Piston

Cylinder

Crankshaft

Running on explosions

A car engine works by making petrol explode inside a cylinder. The hot gas inside the cylinder expands, and forces the piston down.

Fuel

Liquid oxygen

Combustion chamber

Electric motors

When an electric current flows in a wire, tiny electrons move through it. If the wire is between 2 magnets, it will move when the current flows. An electric motor has a coil of wires that keeps turning inside a strong magnetic field.

Coil

Magnet

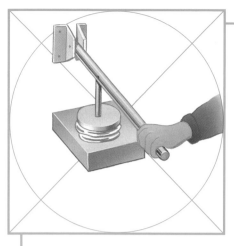

LIGHTENING THE LOAD

Unless you are unusually strong, you will not be able to crack a nut with your bare hands. But with a pair of nutcrackers, the job is straightforward. They alter the way that the work has to be done, using levers to magnify the force that you can exert, so your hand moves much further. Many of the devices that we use every day work in this way, trading the force that is exerted with the distance that has to be moved.

Levers in the body
Your lower jaw is a living lever. Like all levers, it rotates around a hinge called a fulcrum. The back of your jaw is nearest the fulcrum. It travels a small distance, but has a very powerful bite. The front of the jaw travels further, and cannot bite so strongly.

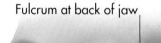
Fulcrum at back of jaw

Force of jaws

Light work
A wheelbarrow makes it easy to lift a heavy object. The handles move upwards much further than the weight.

Force on handles

Fulcrum

Getting a grip
Pliers and scissors have long handles, and short 'jaws'. The handles move a long distance, with a small force. The jaws move less, with a greater force.

Racket moves much further than hand, but with reduced force

Fulcrum (wrist)

Smashing lever
A tennis racket is a lever that increases the distance moved, and reduces force. It moves very quickly to smash the ball over the net.

10

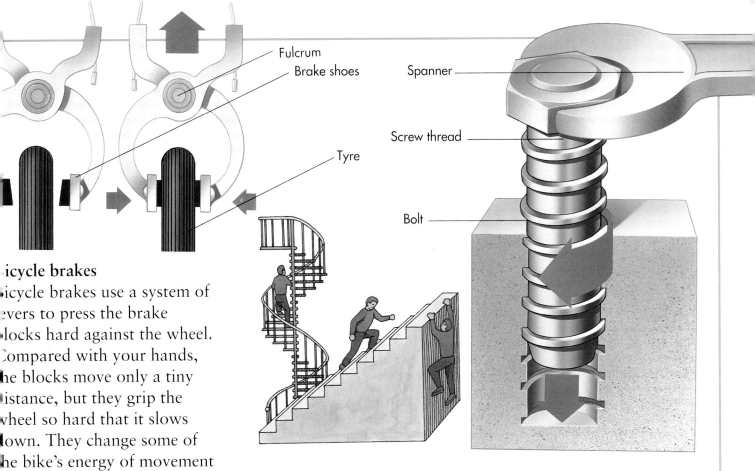

Fulcrum
Brake shoes
Spanner
Screw thread
Tyre
Bolt

Bicycle brakes

Bicycle brakes use a system of levers to press the brake blocks hard against the wheel. Compared with your hands, the blocks move only a tiny distance, but they grip the wheel so hard that it slows down. They change some of the bike's energy of movement into heat.

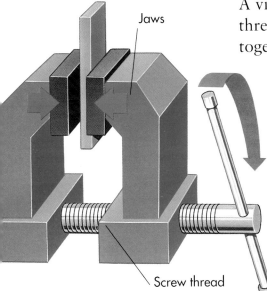

Jaws

In the grip of a vice

A vice uses a very long screw thread to bring 2 jaws together. It takes many turns of the handle to move the jaws a small way, but they come together with great force. The long handle works like a lever, to give the jaws an even tighter grip. Long screw threads are used in many car jacks, enabling a driver to lift a car alone.

Screw thread

Taking the easy route

Although you have to walk further, climbing stairs takes less effort than the equivalent vertical climb. A bolt works like a spiral staircase, with a sloping thread that winds around it.

Hand wheel

Stopping the flow

The water that comes out of a tap is under great pressure. A tap uses a screw thread to counteract the pressure, and control the flow. The thread moves a rubber washer, which lifts up to let water out, or moves down to shut it off.

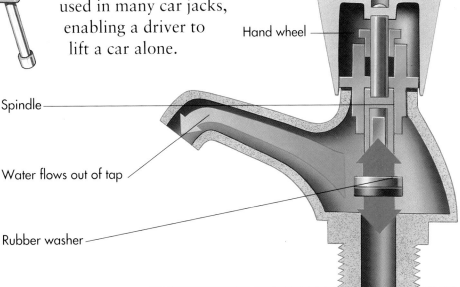

Spindle

Water flows out of tap

Rubber washer

WHEELS

The wheel was invented over 5,000 years ago. In those days, wheels were not used for moving about. Instead, they were used to spin slabs of clay to be shaped into pots. A potter's wheel turns horizontally and stays in one place. But soon people found that this wheel could also be used upright, to make things roll along. Since then, wheels have become an essential part of many machines. Wheels and bearings work by reducing friction, the force that opposes movement when one object slides over another.

Rolling along
Before wheels were used for moving, people shifted heavy objects on wooden rollers. Rollers reduce friction, but they have to be picked up and moved as the load slides along.

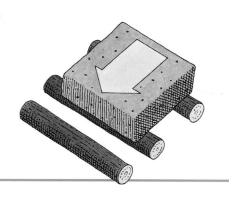

Wheels on the move
The first cartwheels were solid, and very heavy. Spokes were invented about 4,000 years ago.

Losing weight
A bicycle wheel is strong but light. Its spokes pull against the rim and keep it in shape.

Propeller
A propeller turns on an axle, like a wheel. Instead of rolling forwards, it turns sideways. Its blades cut through water, and are angled to push the water backwards. This produces a reaction – an equal and opposite force – which drives the boat forwards.

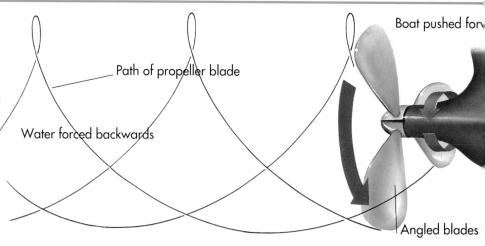

Boat pushed forw

Path of propeller blade

Water forced backwards

Angled blades

Reducing friction

When a wheel turns round, friction slows it down. Friction occurs between the wheel and the ground, and also between the wheel and its axle. Ball bearings reduce friction between wheels and axles. Like rollers, they cut down the areas in contact with each other. Each bearing is made up by a ring of steel balls.

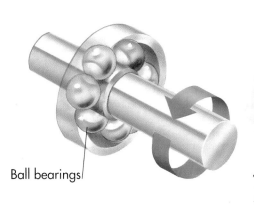

Ball bearings

Bearings at work
To see how bearings reduce friction, roll a tray over some marbles. It slides over easily.

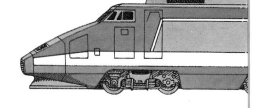

Air-filled tyres
Cars run on pneumatic tyres, which are filled with air. They absorb bumps in the road.

Spreading the load
A tractor's tyres have a large surface area. This stops them sinking in soft ground.

Running on metal
A train's wheels are made of solid metal. An inner flange keeps the wheel on the rail.

Power from water
A turbine is like a propeller that works in reverse. Instead of turning and pushing something, it is pushed, and this makes it turn. Hydroelectric turbines harness the energy of moving water, to generate electricity.

Turbine

High water level

Low water level

Water flow

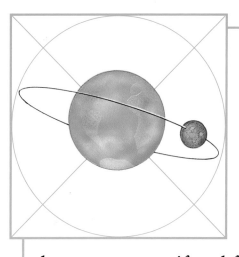

TURNING IN A CIRCLE

If you tie a weight to a piece of string and whirl the weight around, the string becomes tight. But when you slow down and stop, the string slackens. This is because the weight tries to keep moving in a straight line, while the string makes it change direction. The result is a pull, known as centrifugal force, that seems to work outwards from the centre of the circle. Once things start to spin, they are also very hard to turn in a new direction. This principle, too, is used in machines.

Washing machines

A washing machine contains a hollow inner drum turned by an electric motor. When the machine is washing, the drum turns slowly, so that the clothes keep tumbling into the water. But when the wash has finished, the drum speeds up, so that it turns several hundred times a minute. Centrifugal force throws the water and clothes outwards, and the water escapes through small holes, and is then pumped away.

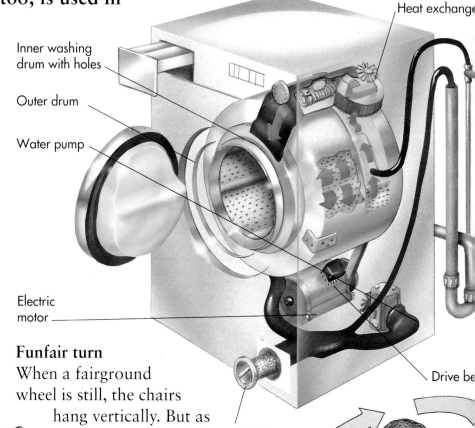

Inner washing drum with holes

Outer drum

Water pump

Electric motor

Heat exchange

Fluff filter

Drive be

Funfair turn

When a fairground wheel is still, the chairs hang vertically. But as soon as it gathers speed, the chairs are thrown outwards by centrifugal force. The faster the wheel turns, the higher the chairs lift up. A similar thing happens if you swing a bucket containing water.

A steady spin

When something spins quickly, it is hard to alter the direction of its spin. This is why a rapidly spinning coin can balance on edge, and why it falls over when it slows down. It also explains why it is easy to keep a bicycle upright when its wheels are turning quickly, but not when they are turning slowly. The same effect helps to stop a heavy motorbike falling over as it races around a corner.

...ancing trick

...yroscope makes an ...resting toy, but it is also an ...ortant part of instruments ...d for navigation. It contains ...eavy wheel that spins ...und an axle. The wheel ...ps the axle pointing in a ...stant direction, so it can ...ance on a string or even on ... tip of a pencil. In an ...raft, gyroscopes spinning ...ight-angles show which ...y the plane is pointing.

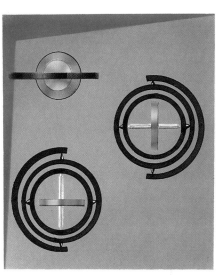

Three gyroscopes at right-angles show a plane's angle and direction

...iming true

... rifle has spiral grooves on ...e inside of its barrel. As the ...ullet travels down the barrel, ...e grooves make it spin very ...uickly. This spin keeps the

bullet moving in a constant direction, although it is still pulled downwards by gravity. A bullet that did not spin

could veer off from a straight path. Bigger guns, which fire shells, have spiral barrels too.

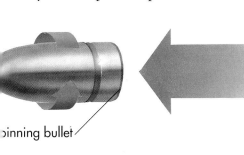

...pinning bullet

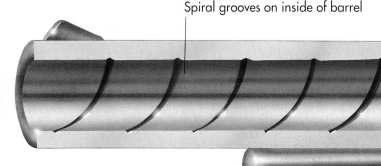

Spiral grooves on inside of barrel

GEARS

Like an engine, your body works better at some speeds than at others. If you pedal a bicycle, you will find that one pace suits you best. But it's not always easy to keep to the same pace. If you go up a hill, you cannot help slowing down. If you go down a slope, you tend to speed up. Gears are a way around this problem. They alter the distance that the wheels move when you turn the pedals, so that you can keep pedalling with a fairly constant force.

Pedal power
When you push on a pedal, your muscle power is carried to the back wheel. The pedals are attached to long levers, called cranks, which enable you to turn the front gear wheel with force. Choosing the right gear lets you either increase the force of the back wheel and reduce its movement, or increase its movement and reduce its force. Gears don't give you extra energy, but they make pedalling easier.

Making connections
The chain carries movement to the rear gear wheels. Because it is made of metal, it does not waste any energy through stretching.

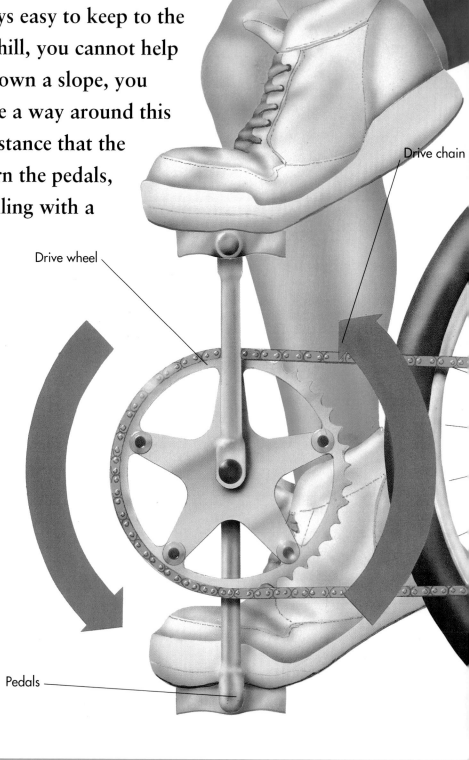

Drive chain

Drive wheel

Pedals

Derailleur gears

In Derailleur gears, the chain can be moved sideways across the rear gear wheels. A small rear gear wheel turns the back wheel fast; a large one turns it slowly, but with force.

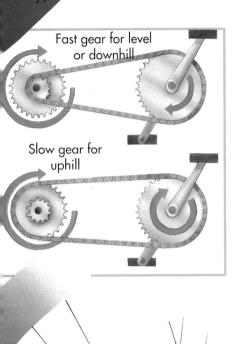

Fast gear for level or downhill

Slow gear for uphill

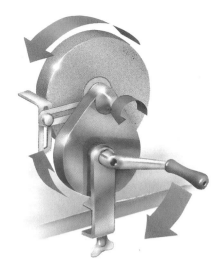

Worm gear

A worm gear has a shaft with a screw thread, and a toothed wheel connected with it. The wheel turns slowly, but with force. Worm gears are often driven by electric motors. which turn very quickly.

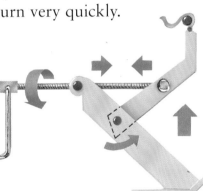

Speeding things up

A grindstone has to turn quickly. Its handle is connected to a large gear with many teeth. This turns a smaller gear, which has fewer teeth. The small gear rotates much faster than the large one. Together, the 2 gears increase speed but reduce force.

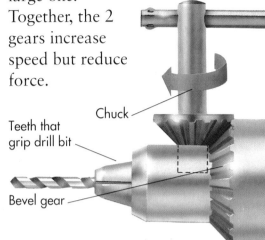

Chuck

Teeth that grip drill bit

Bevel gear

Getting a grip

A drill bit is held in place by 3 metal teeth, which have to grip it very tightly. The teeth are opened or closed by a screw mechanism inside the chuck.

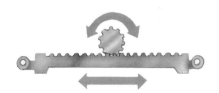

Car gears

A car's gearbox contains several sets of gear wheels on 2 different axles. In each gear, the movement is carried by a different combination of gear wheels.

Slow but sure

A rack and pinion train has a gear wheel, or pinion, gripping a toothed rack. The train can go up steep slopes without slipping.

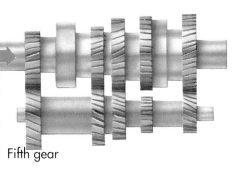

Fifth gear

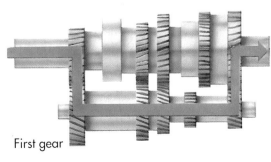

First gear

PUMPS AND PRESSURE

The Earth has a very thick atmosphere which presses against everything on its surface. For example, it presses down on an ordinary chair with a force equivalent to the weight of about 10 people. Fortunately, it also presses upwards with an equal force, so the chair stays in one piece. But pressures are not always equal. Many machines squeeze gases or liquids so that their pressure is different from that of their surroundings. Once substance has been put under pressure like this, it can then be set to work.

Keeping air in

The air inside a bicycle tyre is under much greater pressure than the atmosphere outside. But when you pump up the tyre, the valve stops the air inside rushing out. The valve has a flexible flap that is pushed open by high-pressure air from the pump. As soon as you stop pumping, the air inside pushes against the flap, and makes it close.

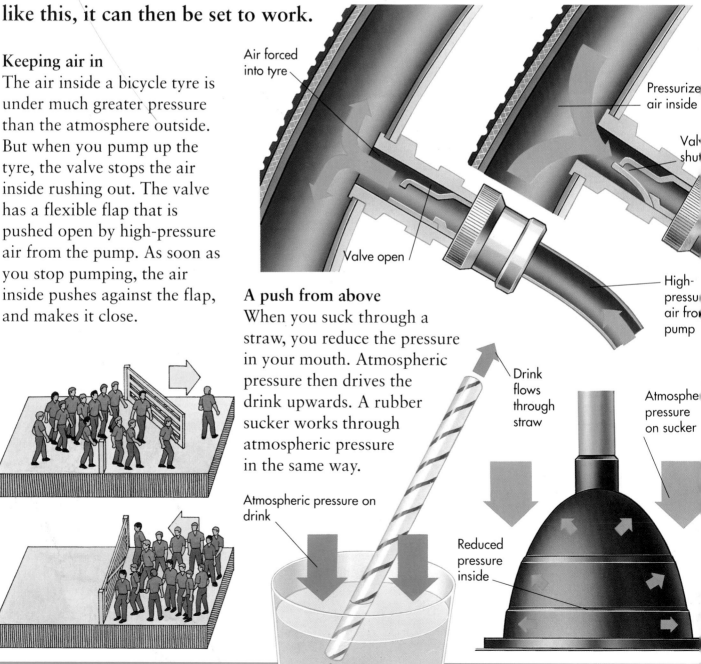

Air forced into tyre

Valve open

Pressurize air inside

Val shu

High-pressu air fro pump

A push from above

When you suck through a straw, you reduce the pressure in your mouth. Atmospheric pressure then drives the drink upwards. A rubber sucker works through atmospheric pressure in the same way.

Drink flows through straw

Atmosphe pressure on sucker

Atmospheric pressure on drink

Reduced pressure inside

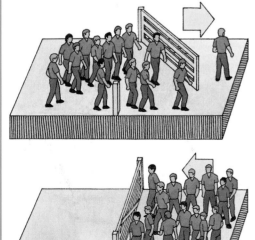

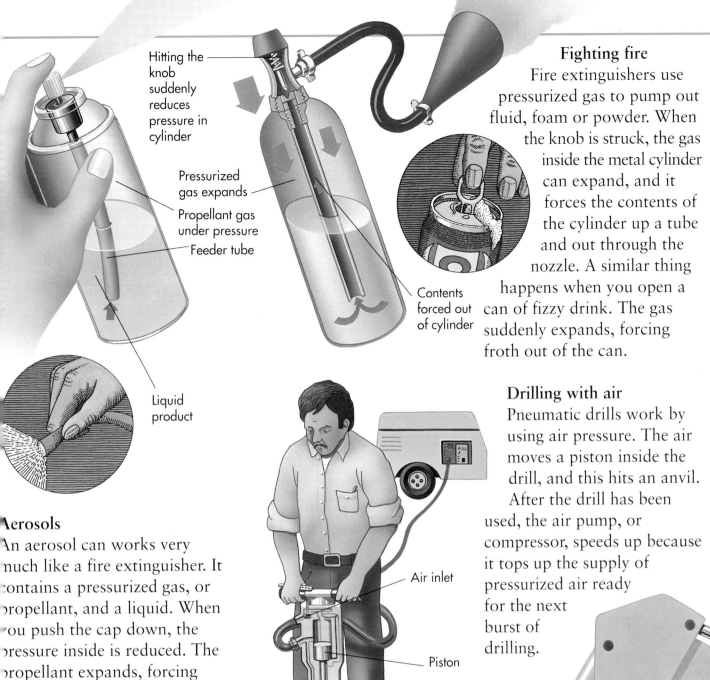

Hitting the knob suddenly reduces pressure in cylinder

Pressurized gas expands

Propellant gas under pressure

Feeder tube

Liquid product

Contents forced out of cylinder

Fighting fire

Fire extinguishers use pressurized gas to pump out fluid, foam or powder. When the knob is struck, the gas inside the metal cylinder can expand, and it forces the contents of the cylinder up a tube and out through the nozzle. A similar thing happens when you open a can of fizzy drink. The gas suddenly expands, forcing froth out of the can.

Drilling with air

Pneumatic drills work by using air pressure. The air moves a piston inside the drill, and this hits an anvil. After the drill has been used, the air pump, or compressor, speeds up because it tops up the supply of pressurized air ready for the next burst of drilling.

Air inlet

Piston

Anvil

Hydraulic fluid

Movement in piston

Icing syringe

Movement of bucket

Water in pipe

Icing syringe

Aerosols

An aerosol can works very much like a fire extinguisher. It contains a pressurized gas, or propellant, and a liquid. When you push the cap down, the pressure inside is reduced. The propellant expands, forcing the liquid outwards. It travels up a narrow nozzle, which makes it break up into very fine spray, like water when you pinch the end of a hose.

Hydraulic power

If you connect 2 icing syringes with some piping in a bowl of water, you have a simple hydraulic system. When one syringe is pushed in, the other moves out. This is because liquids cannot be squashed. If you push them out of one place,

they have to flow to another. A mechanical excavator uses this principle to carry power from one place to another. Its pistons force fluid along strong tubes, and the moving fluid operates other pistons.

LIFTS AND PULLEYS

Everything on the Earth's surface is held in place by gravity. Gravity is actually a very weak force, but because the Earth is enormous, its gravitational pull is very strong. Every time you pick something up, you have to overcome this pull before the object will move. Many devices and machines are designed to help us lift things, or to carry them from one place to another.

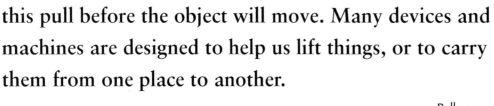

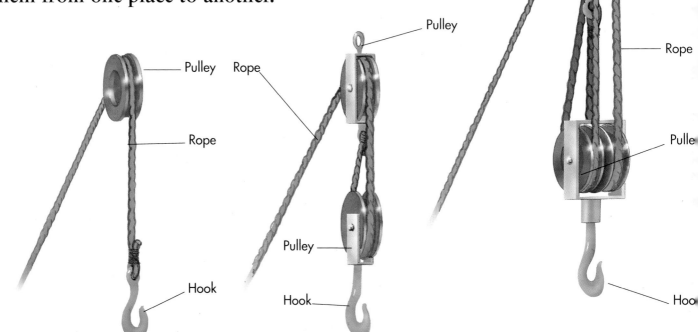

Pulley

Rope

Pulley

Rope

Hook

Pulley

Rope

Pulley

Hook

Pulley

Rope

Pulley

Hook

Single pulley
It is easier to pull down than up. A single pulley lets you use your weight to lift something.

Double pulley
In a double pulley, the lower pulley moves only half as far as the rope. But it has more force.

Block and tackle
With a block and tackle, the rope must be pulled a long way to lift the lower pulleys, but they have great force.

Winching a rope
A ship's winch is used to haul ropes, and to pull the ship into its moorings. The winch pulls by friction, rather like a pencil winding string. The rope loops around the winch 2 or 3 times which stops the rope slipping.

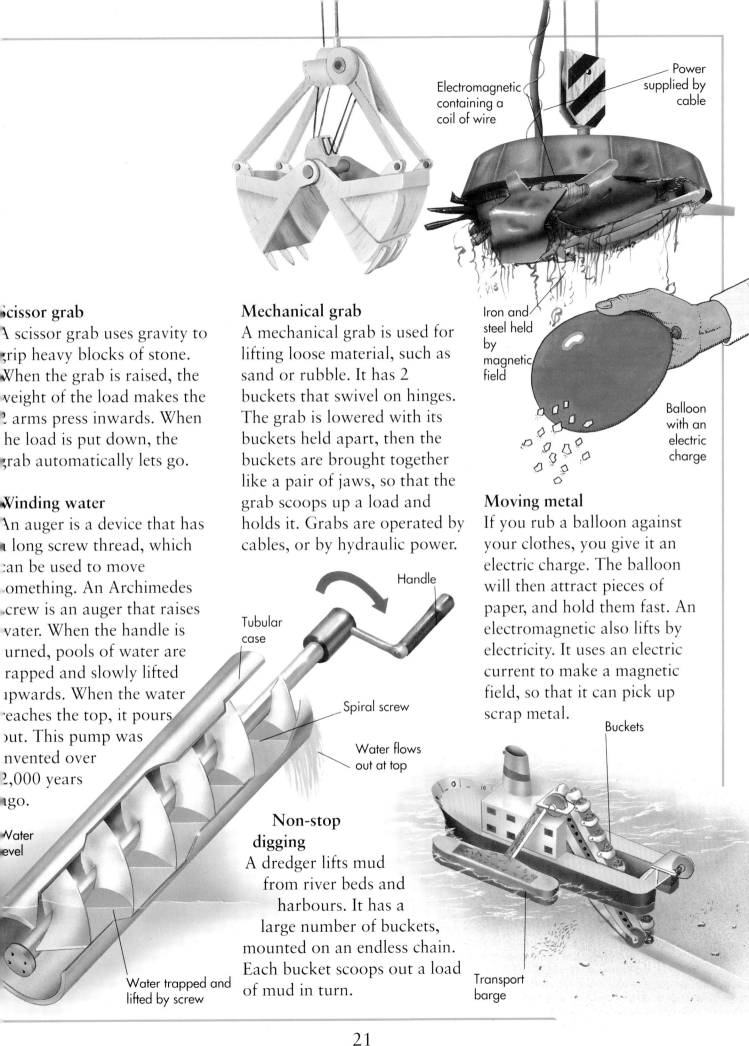

Scissor grab

A scissor grab uses gravity to grip heavy blocks of stone. When the grab is raised, the weight of the load makes the 2 arms press inwards. When the load is put down, the grab automatically lets go.

Winding water

An auger is a device that has a long screw thread, which can be used to move something. An Archimedes screw is an auger that raises water. When the handle is turned, pools of water are trapped and slowly lifted upwards. When the water reaches the top, it pours out. This pump was invented over 2,000 years ago.

Water level

Water trapped and lifted by screw

Mechanical grab

A mechanical grab is used for lifting loose material, such as sand or rubble. It has 2 buckets that swivel on hinges. The grab is lowered with its buckets held apart, then the buckets are brought together like a pair of jaws, so that the grab scoops up a load and holds it. Grabs are operated by cables, or by hydraulic power.

Handle

Tubular case

Spiral screw

Water flows out at top

Non-stop digging

A dredger lifts mud from river beds and harbours. It has a large number of buckets, mounted on an endless chain. Each bucket scoops out a load of mud in turn.

Electromagnetic containing a coil of wire

Power supplied by cable

Iron and steel held by magnetic field

Balloon with an electric charge

Moving metal

If you rub a balloon against your clothes, you give it an electric charge. The balloon will then attract pieces of paper, and hold them fast. An electromagnetic also lifts by electricity. It uses an electric current to make a magnetic field, so that it can pick up scrap metal.

Buckets

Transport barge

21

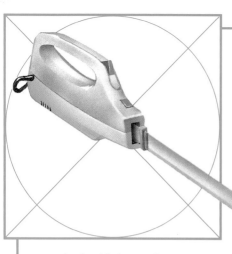

CUTTING

Cutting tools are made from many different materials, to match them to the work that they have to do. Steel is hard enough to cut through paper or wood, but it cannot cut through concrete or rock. For this, blades and drill bits have to be reinforced with other metals, such as tungsten, or with pieces of diamond, the hardest known substance.

Combine harvester

At one time, harvesting corn and other grain crops was a slow business. The corn was cut, then the grain was 'threshed', or separated from the rest of the plant. Next, the grain was collected, and the leftover straw cleared away. Today, the whole job can be done in a few hours by a combine harvester. The harvester gathers the plants with a rotating rake. The stalks are sliced by the cutter bar, and the cut plants travel up into the harvester. Here, they are beaten by rotating bars. The grain breaks off and falls through several sieves, while the straw is carried to the back of the machine. When enough grain has been harvested, it is pumped into a truck by an auger (spiral screw).

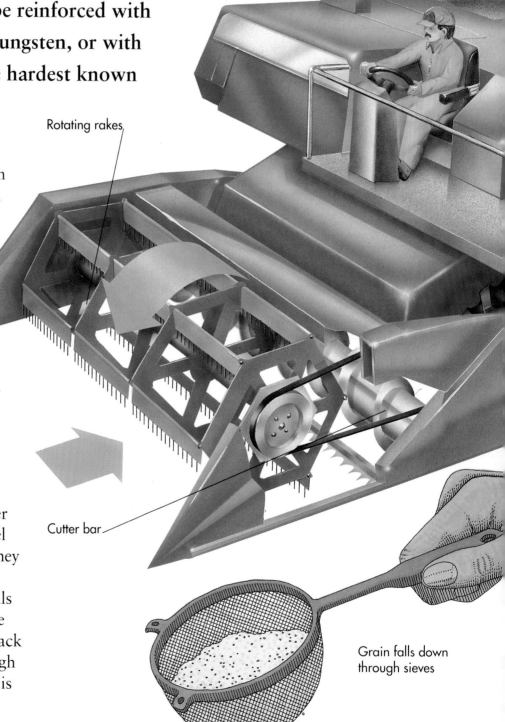

Straw travels through harvester

Rotating rakes

Cutter bar

Grain falls down through sieves

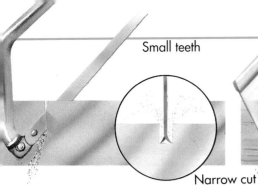

Small teeth

Large teeth

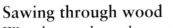
Narrow cut

Wide cut

Short blades widely spaced on chain

Sawing through metal
A hacksaw has a narrow blade with small, very hard teeth. It leaves a narrow cut.

Sawing through wood
Wood saws have large teeth with a sideways curve. They make a wide cut.

The harvester's sieves allow the grains to drop through. The chaff (flakes around the grain) is blown away by a fan.

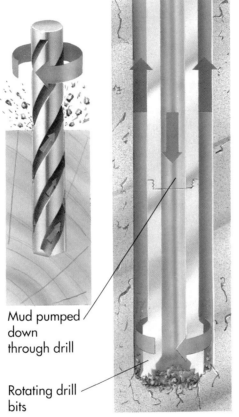

Mud pumped down through drill

Rotating drill bits

Chain saw
A chain saw has short blades that are angled so that they make a wide cut. The bottom half of the chain travels towards the engine, so that the saw pulls away from the operator and digs into the wood.

Cutting in a circle
A drill is a rotating cutting blade. Only the tip does any cutting. In a wood drill, the spirals work like an auger, and carry away the sawdust. In an oil drill, waste rock is carried away by mud pumped up the drill.

Tunnelling machines
Road and rail tunnels are built with giant cutting machines. At the front is the cutter head, a large disc with hard teeth. This head is pushed forward by hydraulic rams, and it slowly rotates, cutting the rock. The loose rock falls through gaps in the cutter.

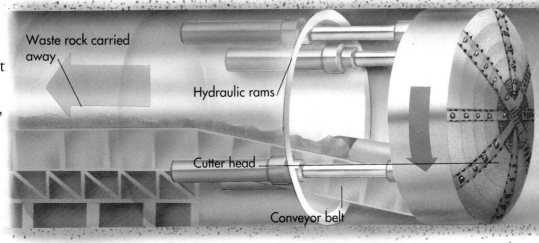

Waste rock carried away

Hydraulic rams

Cutter head

Conveyor belt

HEATING THINGS UP

Everybody knows what heats feels like. But what exactly is it? The answer is pure energy. If something is warm, its atoms have a lot of energy, and they hurtle about very quickly. But if it is cold, they have less energy, and they move only slowly. Heat always flows in one direction. It travels from things that are warmer to things that are cooler. Many machines produce heat and then pass it on, so that it warms up something else.

Instant heat

An instant gas water heater is designed to provide hot water almost as soon as a tap is turned on. The water travels through a heat exchanger, which is a system of pipes connected to metal sheets. The sheets have a large surface area, so they can collect heat from the gas flames rapidly, and carry it to the water.

Heat from electricity

When an electric current flows through a conductor, it generates heat. An electric kettle uses this to boil water. As the water heats, it forms steam which flows past a thermostat. When the water boils, the thermostat switches off the current. An electric kettle is very efficient, almost all the energy it uses is passed on to the water as heat.

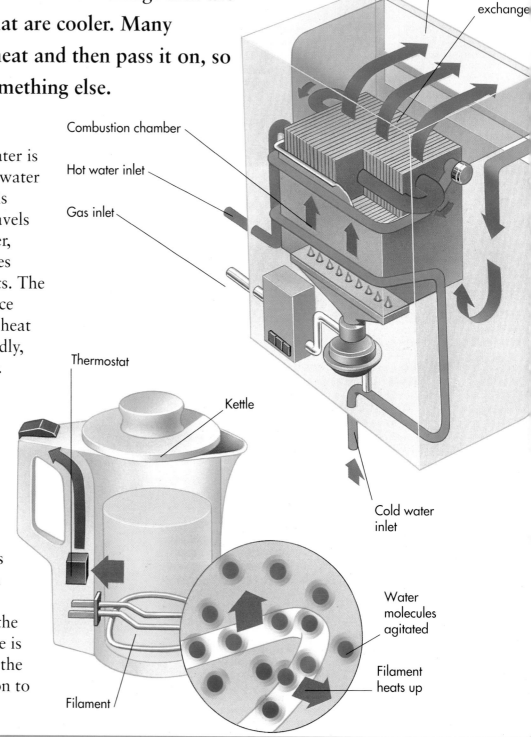

Flue outlet and inlet

Hea exchange

Combustion chamber

Hot water inlet

Gas inlet

Thermostat

Kettle

Cold water inlet

Water molecules agitated

Filament heats up

Filament

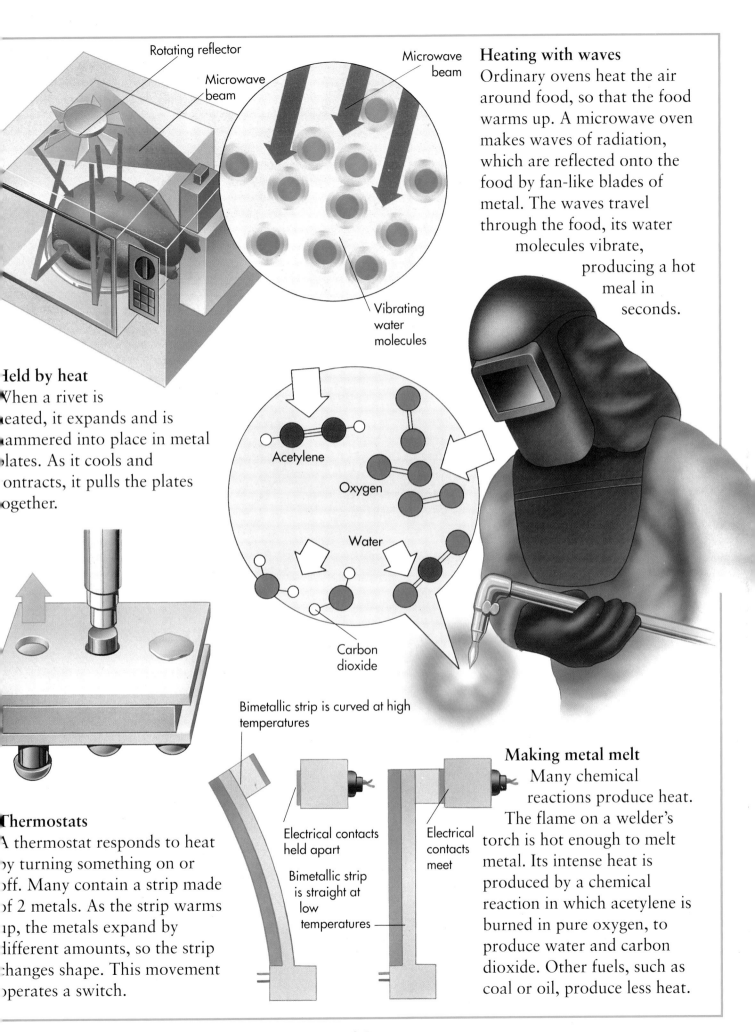

Heating with waves

Ordinary ovens heat the air around food, so that the food warms up. A microwave oven makes waves of radiation, which are reflected onto the food by fan-like blades of metal. The waves travel through the food, its water molecules vibrate, producing a hot meal in seconds.

Rotating reflector

Microwave beam

Microwave beam

Vibrating water molecules

Held by heat

When a rivet is heated, it expands and is hammered into place in metal plates. As it cools and contracts, it pulls the plates together.

Acetylene

Oxygen

Water

Carbon dioxide

Thermostats

A thermostat responds to heat by turning something on or off. Many contain a strip made of 2 metals. As the strip warms up, the metals expand by different amounts, so the strip changes shape. This movement operates a switch.

Bimetallic strip is curved at high temperatures

Electrical contacts held apart

Bimetallic strip is straight at low temperatures

Electrical contacts meet

Making metal melt

Many chemical reactions produce heat. The flame on a welder's torch is hot enough to melt metal. Its intense heat is produced by a chemical reaction in which acetylene is burned in pure oxygen, to produce water and carbon dioxide. Other fuels, such as coal or oil, produce less heat.

COOLING DOWN

Heat can be useful, but sometimes it can be a problem. It cannot be made to disappear, but it can be encouraged to flow away. This is exactly what many machines and devices are designed to do. Fans and cooling fins work by giving heat a chance to escape. Refrigerators and air conditioners work by using heat to evaporate a special liquid. The vapour that this creates carries the heat with it, and when it turns back into a liquid once more, it gives up the heat. By using this principle, refrigerators and air conditioners move heat from one place to another.

Air conditioning

An air conditioner works by sucking in warm air from a room, and blowing it over an evaporator. The evaporator is kept cold by a compressor, in the same way as in a refrigerator. The cooled air is then filtered before being blown back into the room.

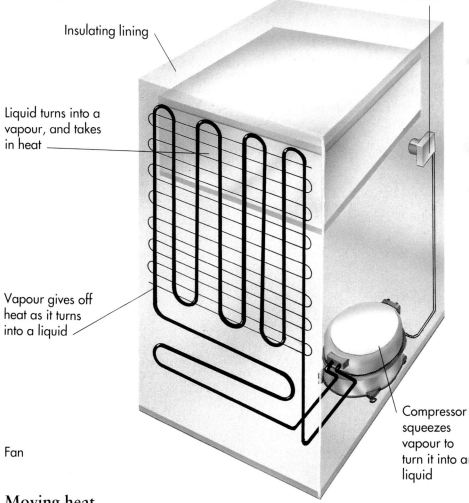

Thermostat

Insulating lining

Liquid turns into a vapour, and takes in heat

Vapour gives off heat as it turns into a liquid

Compressor squeezes vapour to turn it into a liquid

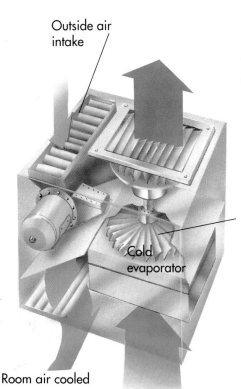

Outside air intake

Fan

Cold evaporator

Room air cooled

Moving heat

A refrigerator's icebox is surrounded by pipes, containing a liquid that evaporates to form a vapour. This takes in heat. The vapour is then pumped through pipes outside the fridge, and squeezed so that it condenses. The vapour turns to liquid again, and loses heat.

drill bit

Cooling fan

Blowing heat away

The motor in an electric drill generates a lot of heat, particularly when it is working hard. If the heat builds up, it can melt the drill's wiring. To prevent this happening, the drill has a built-in fan. The fan blows air over the drill, and the air warms up, carrying away some of the drill's heat. Many electrical machines are cooled by fans.

Letting heat escape

Heat escapes more quickly from a large surface than from a small one. The fins on a motorbike engine use this principle to keep the engine cool. They conduct heat away from the cylinder, and lose it by warming the surrounding air. The faster the motorbike moves, the more air is blown through the fins.

Cooling fins

Air blows through fins

Cooling by air

Most power stations make electricity by blowing steam through turbines. After the steam has been used, it has to be turned back to water again. The steam is cooled by water, and the water is piped through large towers, where it is cooled by a rising current of air. As the air rises, its moisture condenses, and this makes clouds of vapour.

Steam circulates through tower inside pipes

Steam inside the pipes condenses, and returns to power station

Power station

Cold water trickles over pipes, and turns into steam

27

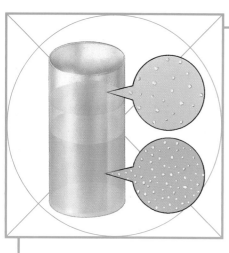

FLOATING

If you pour cooking oil into water, the 2 liquids don't mix. The oil forms a layer that stays on top. This is an example of flotation. It is caused by a difference in densities, meaning that a given volume of oil is lighter than the same volume of water. Things float in liquids, and in gases. Flotation keeps ships on the surface of the sea, and holds balloons up in the air.

On take-off, the balloon is only partly inflated

Gas inside balloon

Air outside balloon

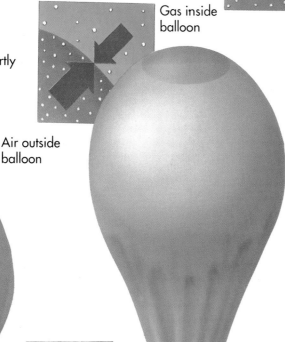

At high altitude, the balloon swells up. It fully inflated, it would burst

As the balloon climbs, the outside pressure drops. The gas inside expands.

Journey through the atmosphere
A high-altitude balloon is filled with helium, a very light gas. The balloon, together with its load, weighs less than the same volume of air at ground level, so it rises.

Full tanker floats low down in water

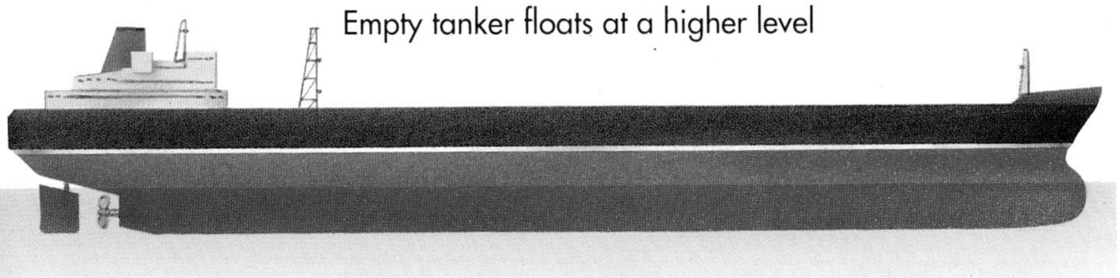

Empty tanker floats at a higher level

Finding a level

Like a bottle, an oil tanker takes up, or 'displaces', its own weight of water. It displaces much more water when it is full, so it floats lower down in the water.

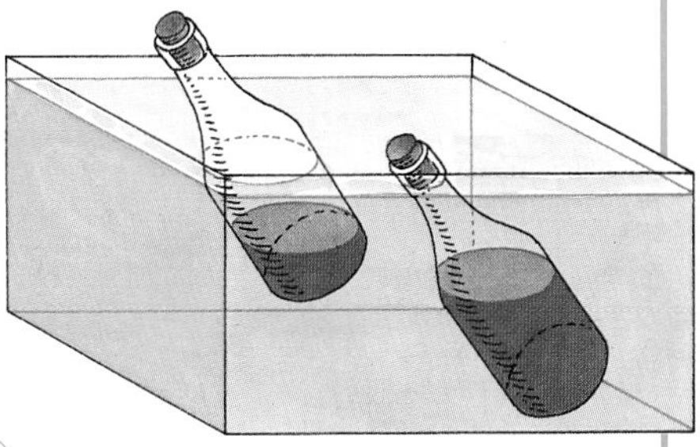

Floating and flying

A hydrofoil combines floating and flying. At slow speeds, it floats on its hull. At high speeds, its foils work like wings, producing an upward force called lift.

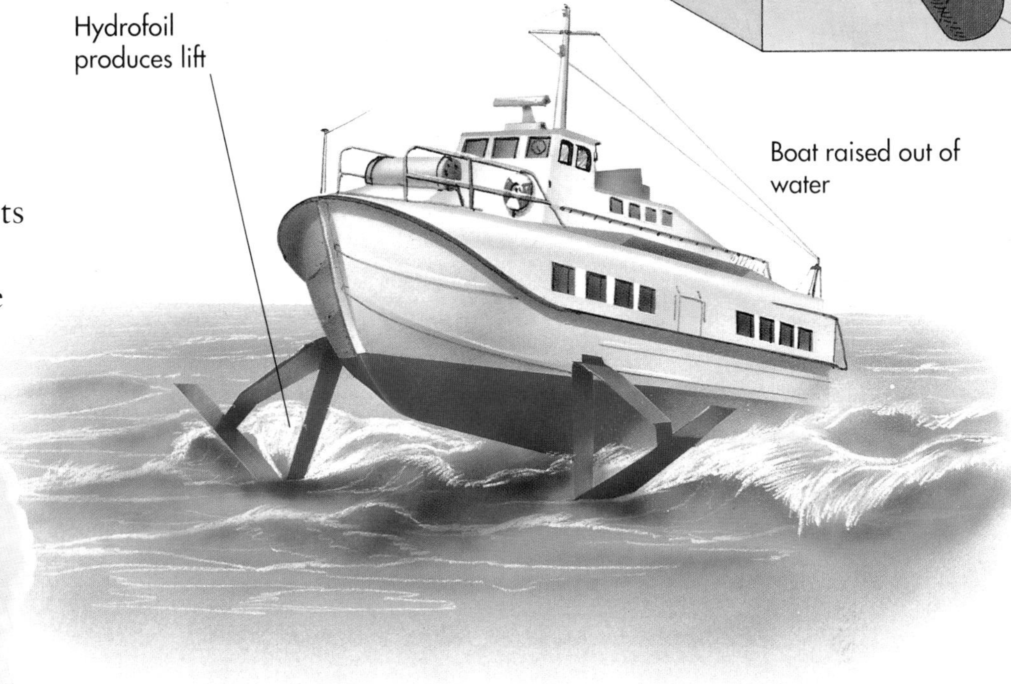

Hydrofoil produces lift

Boat raised out of water

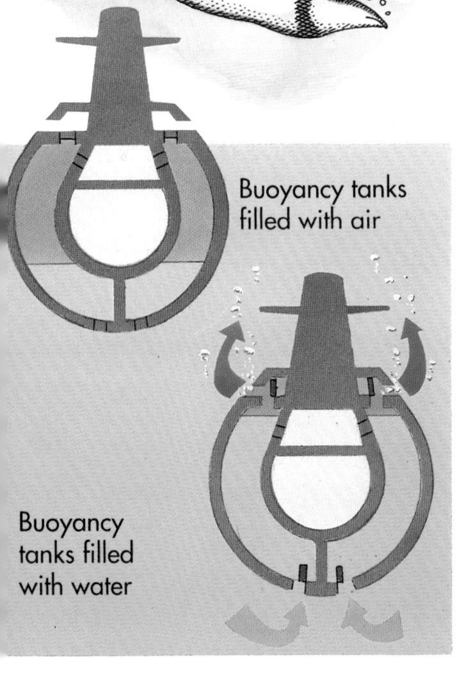

Buoyancy tanks filled with air

Buoyancy tanks filled with water

Changing density

A submarine can float at any level. It does this by changing its density. It has special tanks that can be filled with water, or with air. When they contain air, the sub is less dense than its surroundings, so it rises. When they are flooded with water, it becomes more dense and sinks.

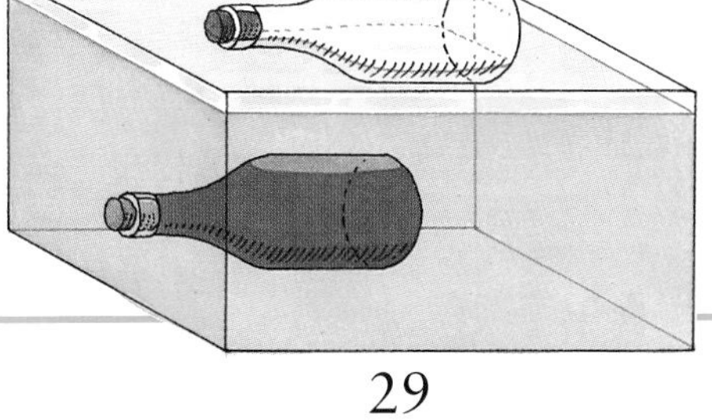

Pressure of the depths

If you dive underwater, you can feel the water pressing against you. Water pressure increases with depth. A deep-sea research vessel has a reinforced chamber built to withstand pressure equal to many tonnes.

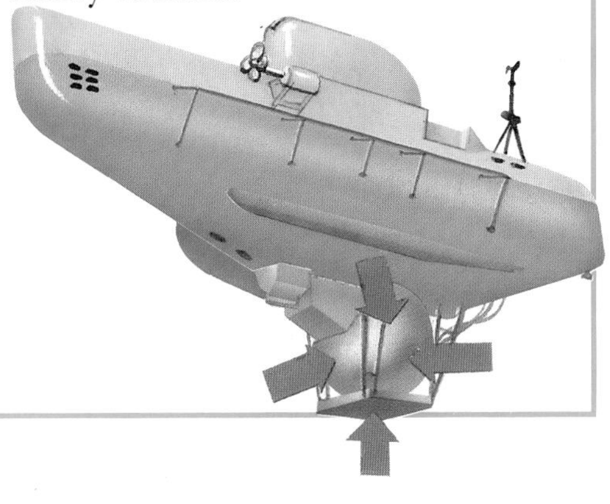

FLYING GLIDING

Birds, planes and helicopters are denser than air, so they cannot stay airborne by floating. They use a force called lift. Lift occurs when air flows over a specially curved surface, called an aerofoil. It pushes the aerofoil up, and counteracts the downward force of gravity. The strength of lift depends on the shape of the aerofoil, and how fast air moves over it. A glider's wings are shaped to produce lift at quite slow speeds.

Streamlined shape reduces drag (friction with air)

Wings at work
Planes that fly at fairly low speeds need a large wing area to generate enough lift. A fighter plane flies faster, so its wing area is less.

In a 'swing wing' plane, the wings can change shape, so the amount of lift can be adjusted to match the speed. Wing flaps called ailerons make a plane roll as it turns.

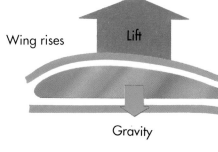

Wing rises — Lift
Gravity

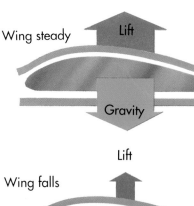

Wing steady — Lift
Gravity

Wing falls — Lift
Gravity

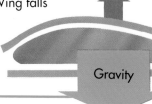

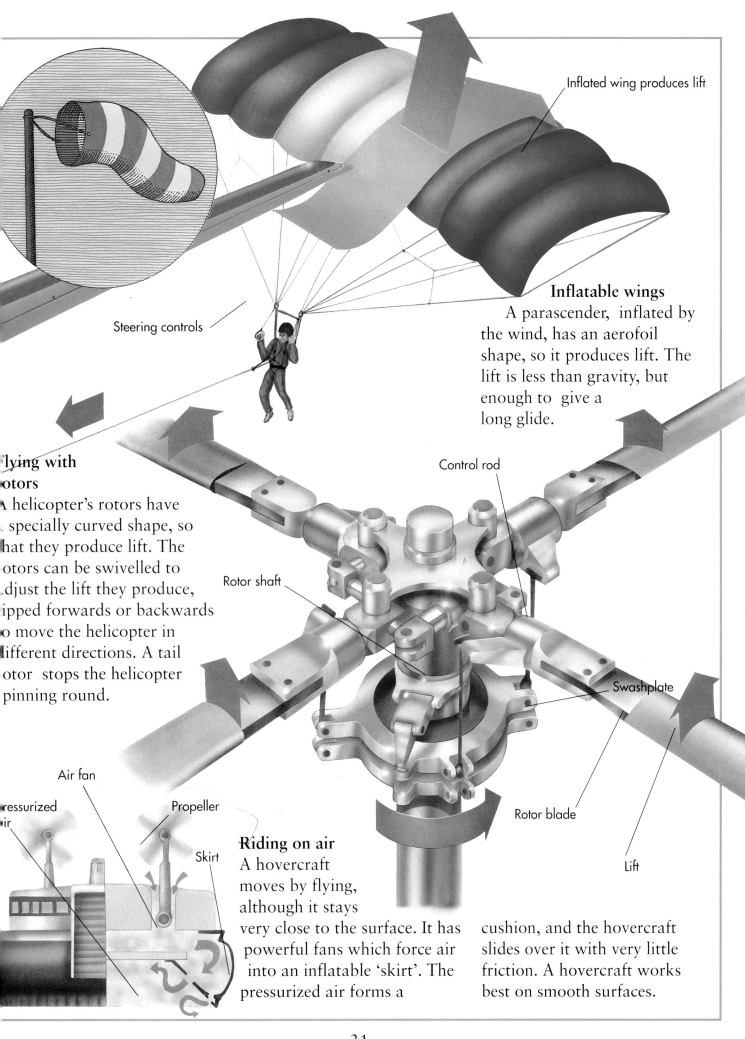

Inflated wing produces lift

Steering controls

Inflatable wings
A parascender, inflated by the wind, has an aerofoil shape, so it produces lift. The lift is less than gravity, but enough to give a long glide.

Control rod

Flying with rotors
A helicopter's rotors have a specially curved shape, so that they produce lift. The rotors can be swivelled to adjust the lift they produce, tipped forwards or backwards to move the helicopter in different directions. A tail rotor stops the helicopter spinning round.

Rotor shaft

Swashplate

Air fan

Pressurized air

Propeller

Skirt

Rotor blade

Lift

Riding on air
A hovercraft moves by flying, although it stays very close to the surface. It has powerful fans which force air into an inflatable 'skirt'. The pressurized air forms a cushion, and the hovercraft slides over it with very little friction. A hovercraft works best on smooth surfaces.

MEASURING

Without help, humans are surprisingly bad at measuring things. It's very difficult for us to guess the exact time or temperature, and hard to judge speeds or distances. Accurate measurements may not seem that important in everyday life, but they are vital for machines. Machine parts have to be made to precise sizes, so that they fit together exactly. Many machines, from ships to aircraft, need exact information about the time, and the conditions around them.

Measuring pressure

A barometer measures the pressure of the atmosphere, which indicates the weather to come. An aneroid barometer contains a metal capsule that has had the air pumped out of it. The sides of the capsule are held apart by a spring. As the air pressure changes, the capsule's sides move in or out moving a needle on a dial.

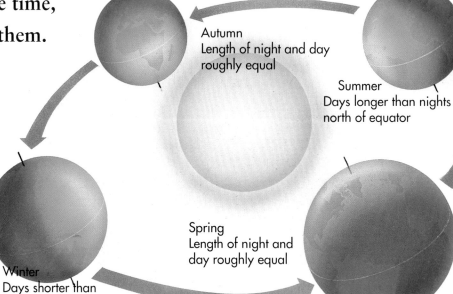

Autumn
Length of night and day roughly equal

Summer
Days longer than nights north of equator

Spring
Length of night and day roughly equal

Winter
Days shorter than nights north of equator

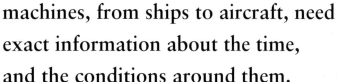

Escapement controls speed of gear wheels

Arm attached to spring

Vacuum capsule

Hairspring

Rocking bar

Measuring time

To measure time, a clock has to contain something that moves at a very exact rate. In clockwork clocks, this is either a swinging pendulum, or a spring that turns first one way, and then another. Modern clocks work electronically, vibrating quartz crystals at a precise frequency.

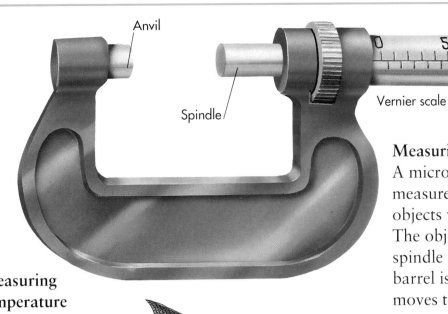

Anvil

Spindle

Vernier scale

Measuring something small

A micrometer is designed to measure the size of small objects with great accuracy. The object is held between the spindle and the anvil. The barrel is then turned, and this moves the spindle forwards on a screw thread. When the object is held tight, its size can be read on the gauge. A special 'Vernier scale' counts fractions of a turn.

Measuring temperature

If you fall ill, your temperature may be taken with a clinical thermometer. Most things expand when they are heated, and a thermometer registers temperatures by measuring this expansion. In a clinical thermometer, the substance that expands is either mercury, a liquid metal, or alcohol. At one end of the thermometer is a small bulb that contains the liquid. When the liquid is warmed by your body's heat, it expands and pushes up a tube connected to the bulb. The hotter you are, the further it travels.

Echo from flying insect

High-pitched sound from bat

Measuring speed

A speedometer shows how fast a car's wheels are turning. Mechanical speedometers do this by using the wheel to turn a cable. The cable spins a magnet, which drags a drum, and the drum turns the needle. Electronic speedometers work by producing a pulse of electricity when the wheel turns.

Measuring length

Our ancestors measured distances with knotted string. Today, an electronic tape measure does this more quickly and accurately. It sends out a beam of high-pitched sound, which bounces back from an object, and the device measures how long it takes to do this. It can then work out the object's distance. Bats use a similar system to detect flying insects.

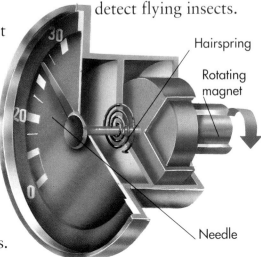

Hairspring

Rotating magnet

Needle

STORING ENERGY

A battery is a package of stored energy. When you switch on a torch, the battery drives an electric current through the bulb, and the energy in the current is converted into light and heat. Batteries are just one way of storing energy. Machines with moving parts often store energy by winding up a spring, or by turning a flywheel. The amount of useful energy that these devices give out is less than the amount that is put in, as some energy is lost as heat.

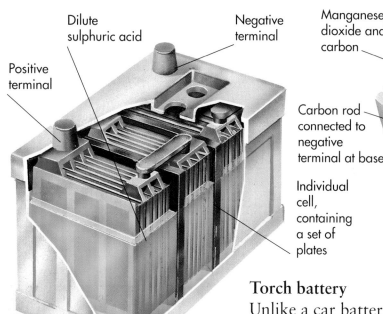

Positive terminal

Dilute sulphuric acid

Negative terminal

Manganese dioxide and carbon

Carbon rod connected to negative terminal at base

Individual cell, containing a set of plates

Ammonium chloride paste

Car battery
A car battery has several sets of lead plates in diluted sulphuric acid. As the battery is charged, electricity flows into it. This drives a chemical reaction, which leaves the 'positive' set of plates coated with oxide. As the battery is used, this is reversed, and electrical energy is given out.

Torch battery
Unlike a car battery, a torch battery does not use a liquid, so it is known as a 'dry cell'. It contains a carbon rod, surrounded by a mix of manganese dioxide and carbon. Outside this is a paste, with ammonium chloride, which conducts electricity. The whole battery is surrounded by a zinc case. When the battery is used, the ammonium chloride reacts with the zinc, which loses electrons, while the carbon rod gains them.

Normally, this reaction would produce bubbles of hydrogen, which could make the battery explode. But the manganese and carbon acts as a 'depolarizer', preventing the hydrogen forming. The voltage of a battery depends on the materials used. This one is about 1.5 volts.

Watch battery

A watch battery is also a 'dry cell', with layers of mercury oxide and powdered zinc, separated by a substance that conducts electricity. Electrons travel from the zinc to the mercury oxide, creating an electrical difference between them of about 1.35 volts.

Energy in springs

If you stretch an elastic band and then let go, it will return to its original size. If you bend a thin strip of metal with a gentle pressure, it will spring back. These are both examples of 'elasticity'. When an elastic object is squeezed or stretched, it stores energy.

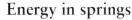

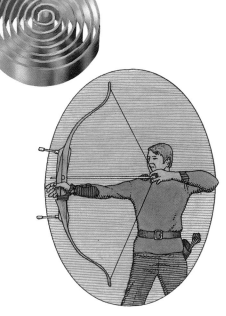

It releases the energy when it regains its original shape. Springs are designed to store lots of energy in this way. They are made of strong steel to withstand a lot of winding or stretching without breaking. Springs are not always metal. A bow is a spring that stores energy and then suddenly releases it to fire an arrow.

Storing heat

A vacuum flask stores energy by making it difficult for heat to get out. It has 2 layers of glass, separated by a space with very little air. Heat cannot flow through here, as there are very few atoms to conduct it. The flask also has a shiny inside surface. This reflects heat rays, and prevents heat escaping.

Smoothing movement

A car's flywheel stores energy from pistons, which produce a jerky movement, and gives it out in a smoother way that makes travelling more comfortable.

Zinc case connected to positive terminal at top of battery

Flywheel

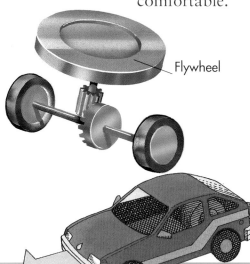

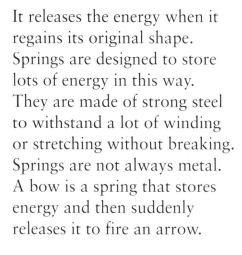
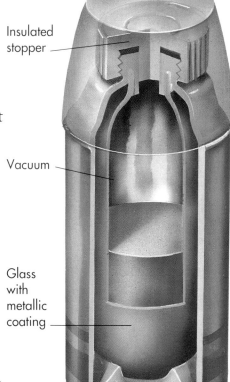

Insulated stopper

Vacuum

Glass with metallic coating

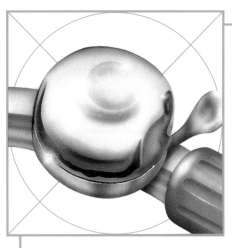

USING SOUND

If you hold a ruler on the edge of a table, and then give the free end a flick, it will make a sound. Sound is a series of vibrations that pass through air. The ruler makes air vibrate by moving up and down, and the faster it moves, the higher is the sound's pitch. Lots of machines make sound, and although they are more complicated than a ruler, they work in much the same way. They have parts that vibrate either at a fixed speed, or at one that can be varied.

Electric bell
An electric bell contains 3 main parts – a bell, a coil of wire, and a metal striker with a springy arm. When the bell is switched on, electricity flows through the coil. This creates a strong magnetic field, which pulls the striker towards it. But as the striker moves towards the coil, it breaks the electric circuit. The magnetic field disappears, and so the striker moves back to its original position. This completes the circuit again, so the sequence of movements starts once more. The striker's rapid action makes the bell ring.

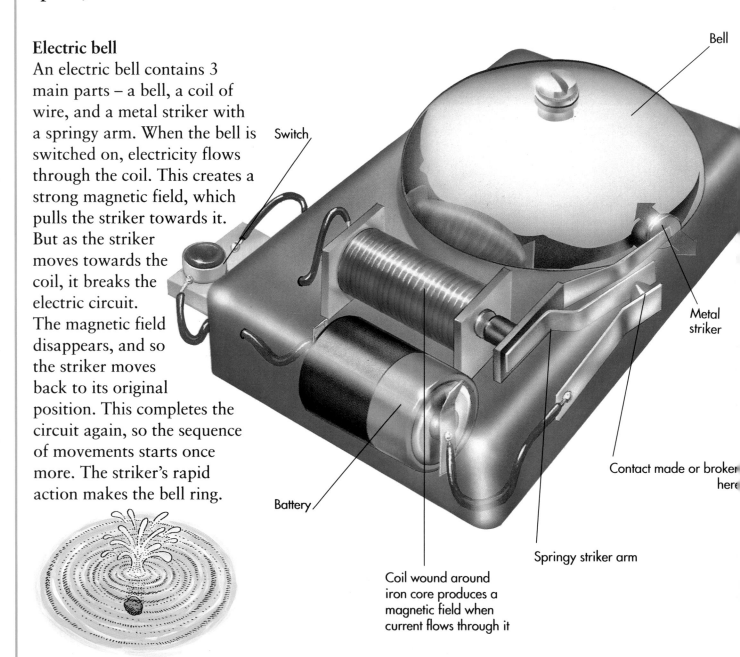

Bell

Switch

Metal striker

Contact made or broken here

Springy striker arm

Coil wound around iron core produces a magnetic field when current flows through it

Battery

Sensing with sound

Sound travels even faster in water than it does in air. An echo sounder, or sonar, probes the sea by sending out bursts of sound, and then timing how long they take to return.

Floating objects, such as fish, reflect the sound sooner than the seabed beneath them. Dolphins use high-pitched sound to locate food, just as bats do in air.

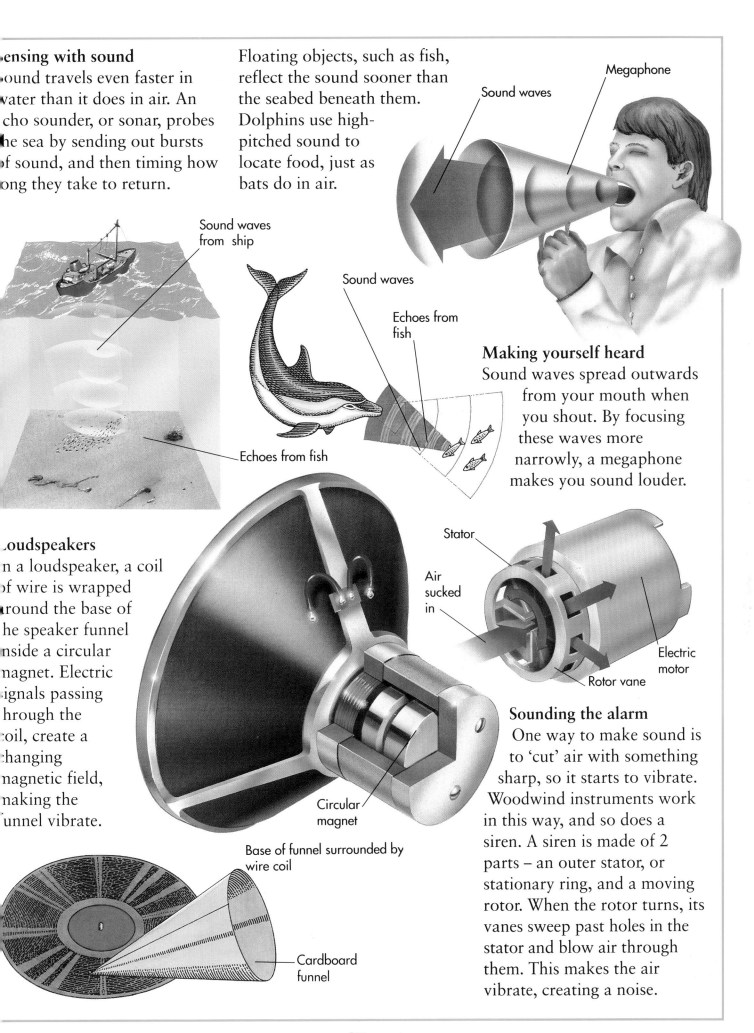

Sound waves

Megaphone

Sound waves from ship

Sound waves

Echoes from fish

Echoes from fish

Making yourself heard
Sound waves spread outwards from your mouth when you shout. By focusing these waves more narrowly, a megaphone makes you sound louder.

Loudspeakers

In a loudspeaker, a coil of wire is wrapped around the base of the speaker funnel inside a circular magnet. Electric signals passing through the coil, create a changing magnetic field, making the funnel vibrate.

Stator

Air sucked in

Electric motor

Rotor vane

Circular magnet

Base of funnel surrounded by wire coil

Cardboard funnel

Sounding the alarm
One way to make sound is to 'cut' air with something sharp, so it starts to vibrate. Woodwind instruments work in this way, and so does a siren. A siren is made of 2 parts – an outer stator, or stationary ring, and a moving rotor. When the rotor turns, its vanes sweep past holes in the stator and blow air through them. This makes the air vibrate, creating a noise.

USING LIGHT

Light energy travels in waves. It always moves in straigh
lines, but it can be bounced by mirrors, and bent by
lenses. Most of the things around you do not make any
light themselves, but
reflect light made
by other objects, such as the Sun, or
electric lightbulbs. When you look
at something, your eyes take in light,
and use it to form an 'image', or
picture of the object.

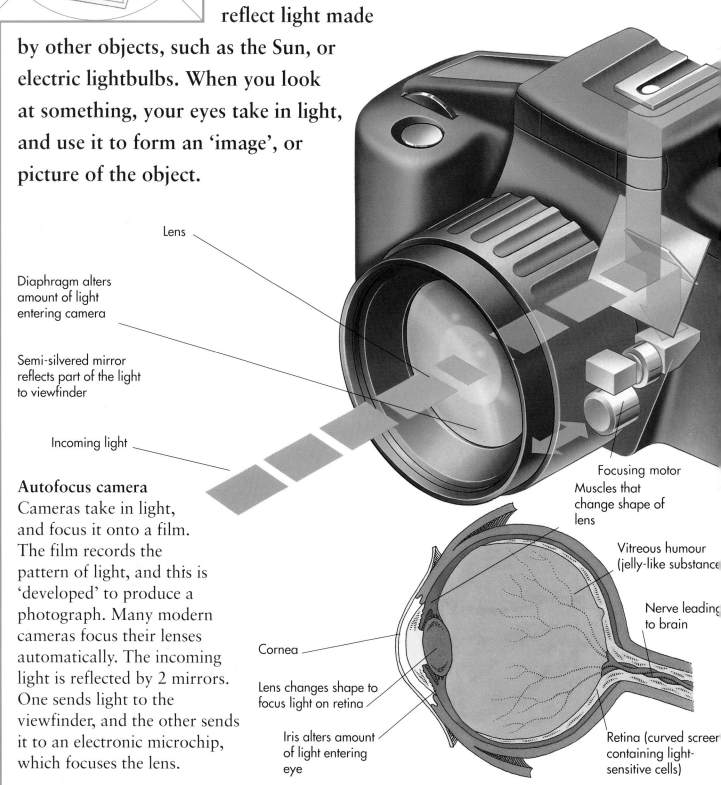

Lens

Diaphragm alters
amount of light
entering camera

Semi-silvered mirror
reflects part of the light
to viewfinder

Incoming light

Focusing motor

Muscles that
change shape of
lens

Vitreous humour
(jelly-like substance

Nerve leading
to brain

Cornea

Lens changes shape to
focus light on retina

Iris alters amount
of light entering
eye

Retina (curved screen
containing light-
sensitive cells)

Autofocus camera
Cameras take in light,
and focus it onto a film.
The film records the
pattern of light, and this is
'developed' to produce a
photograph. Many modern
cameras focus their lenses
automatically. The incoming
light is reflected by 2 mirrors.
One sends light to the
viewfinder, and the other sends
it to an electronic microchip,
which focuses the lens.

Making things bigger

A compound microscope shines light upwards through an object on a slide. The objective lenses form a magnified image of the object inside the barrel of the microscope. The eyepiece lenses then work like a magnifying glass to make the image about 500 times bigger.

Eye

Eyepiece lens

Objective lens

Mirror

Focusing knob

Second prism reflects light backwards

First prism reflects light forwards

Eyepiece lens

Sliding tubes allow image to be focused

Bringing things closer

Telescopes and binoculars work in the same way, but binoculars save space by using prisms to reflect the light. The lenses gather light, and then bend it in sharply. This makes the view seem bigger.

Looking around corners

Looking in a mirror, you see things back-to-front. But if you look around corners with a periscope, they are the right way round. A periscope has 2 mirrors. The first reverses light rays, the second puts them back the right way.

Incoming light

First mirror

Light bent through 90

Second mirror

Cutting by light

Daylight is a jumble of wavelengths, but laser light has just one wavelength. All the waves move in step.

Waves of ordinary light

Waves of laser light

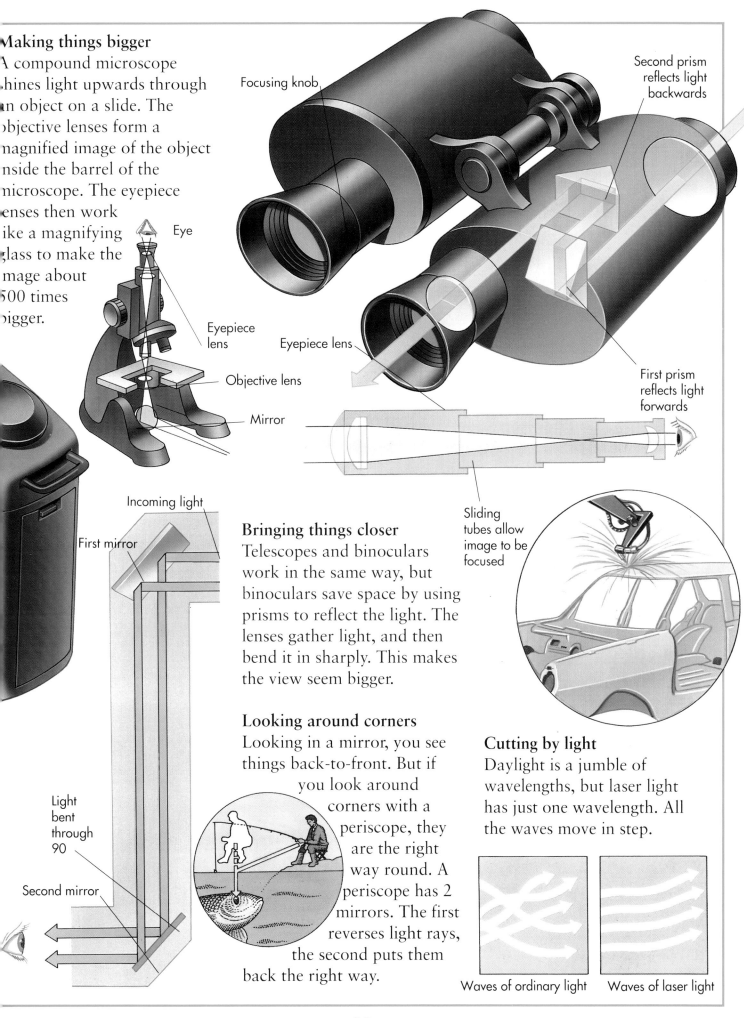

SENDING SIGNALS

In 1888, Heinrich Hertz discovered radio waves, an invisible form of energy that travels at the speed of light. People soon found that radio waves could be interrupted or altered to make them carry signals across distances, without any wires or cables being needed. Today, our planet is bristling with radio waves of many different lengths, or frequencies. Some carry signals that radios convert into sounds. Others carry signals that TV sets build into pictures.

Making a picture

A television collects radio signals and uses them to trigger 3 electron guns which make the screen give off light. The guns send out electrons, which are bent by magnetic coils so that they strike the screen in just the right places at the right time. If you look closely at a television picture, you will see that it is made up of tiny strips of red, green and blue. A special mask makes sure that each beam lights up strips of just one colour, and together the colours form the picture. The screen makes a new picture 50 times every second. The pictures are still, but so close together they seem to move.

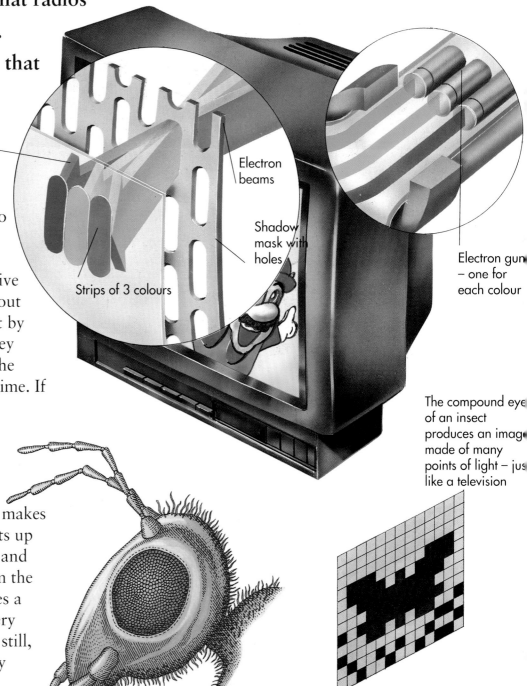

Glass screen

Strips of 3 colours

Electron beams

Shadow mask with holes

Electron gun – one for each colour

The compound eye of an insect produces an image made of many points of light – just like a television

Satellite communications

Radio waves usually travel in straight lines, although they can be bent and reflected by different layers in the atmosphere. A satellite collects radio waves from a transmitter on the ground, and then reflects them back over a wide area. The reflected waves are collected by a special parabolic dish, which focuses them on to a receiver.

From signals to sound

A radio aerial responds to radio waves by producing a weak electrical signal. The radio amplifies the signal so that it is strong enough to drive a loudspeaker (p.36). Radio waves arrive almost instantly, travelling at the speed of light (300,000 km/h).

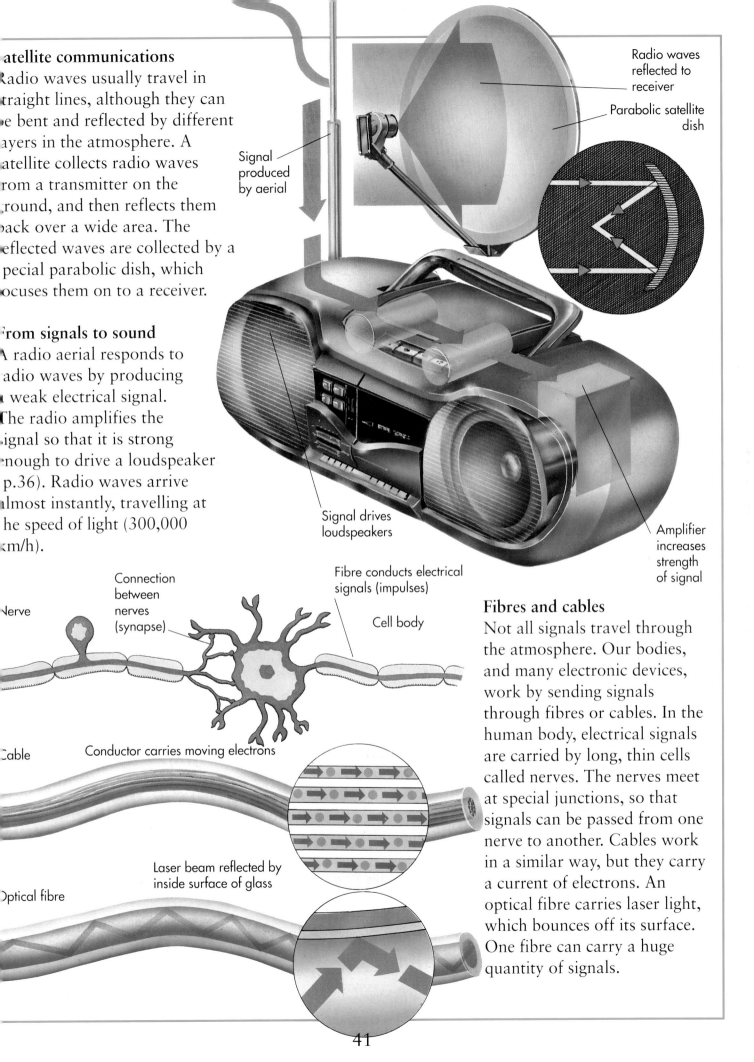

Radio waves reflected to receiver

Parabolic satellite dish

Signal produced by aerial

Signal drives loudspeakers

Amplifier increases strength of signal

Nerve

Connection between nerves (synapse)

Fibre conducts electrical signals (impulses)

Cell body

Cable

Conductor carries moving electrons

Optical fibre

Laser beam reflected by inside surface of glass

Fibres and cables

Not all signals travel through the atmosphere. Our bodies, and many electronic devices, work by sending signals through fibres or cables. In the human body, electrical signals are carried by long, thin cells called nerves. The nerves meet at special junctions, so that signals can be passed from one nerve to another. Cables work in a similar way, but they carry a current of electrons. An optical fibre carries laser light, which bounces off its surface. One fibre can carry a huge quantity of signals.

41

MEMORY MACHINES

Information is something that we use all the time. The words in this book contain information, as do pictures, computer programs, and even pieces of music. Storing words or pictures on a page is quite easy, although it takes up quite a lot of space. Electronic machines store information in a much more compact way, either by using magnetism, or by using light. At the touch of a button, the machine converts the information into a form that we can understand.

Magnetic tapes

A tape is a ribbon of plastic with a magnetic coating. When sound is recorded, it is converted into electrical signals. These are sent to an electromagnet, which magnetizes particles on the tape. When the tape plays, the particles create a current, amplified to produce the sound.

Analogue and digital

In an analogue tape recording, the information is stored as a continuous stream of magnetism, which varies in step with the signal. But in a digital tape recording, the information is stored as millions of separate patches of magnetism. The patches work like a code, and the machine 'reads' the code to make the sounds or pictures. Digital recordings give a very clear sound, because the code is very precise.

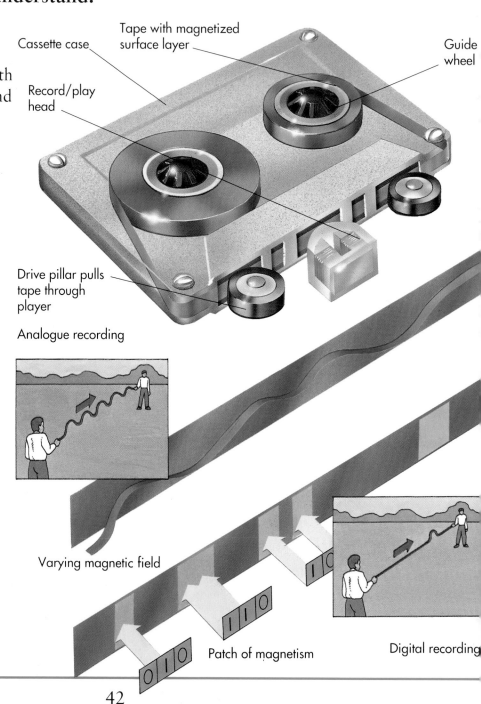

Cassette case

Tape with magnetized surface layer

Guide wheel

Record/play head

Drive pillar pulls tape through player

Analogue recording

Varying magnetic field

Patch of magnetism

Digital recording

Compact disc

A compact disc player is a digital machine. Instead of storing information by magnetism, it stores it as a series of microscopic pits. As the disc spins around, a laser beam shines onto its lower surface. The beam detects the sequence of pits, and the player uses this information to assemble a sound or picture. To play just 1 minute of music, the player reads and decodes a sequence of over 2 million pits. The pits also hold other information. This enables the player to check that it is working properly, and allows it to locate individual tracks.

Computer disc

Areas of magnetism on disc

Read/write head moved by electric motor

Floppy disc

A floppy disc is a form of magnetic storage used by computers. It works like a tape, but instead of winding the disc back and forth to get to a piece of information, the computer can move across the disc to reach any point. This is called 'random access'. It allows the computer to handle information fast. The computer divides the disc into separate sectors. It keeps a record of what is in each one, so it can quickly move its read/write head to the right place.

Direction of disc

Credit cards

The black strip on the back of a credit card holds details, like an account number, in magnetic form. When the card is put in a machine, it reads this information.

Credit card with magentic strip

Close-up of underside of a compact disc, showing pits

Tiny pits create a colour pattern, like the scales on a butterfly's wing

Strips marking code

9 780749 60703 6

Beam reflected by pits on disc

Laser

Beam passes back through mirror

Semi-reflecting mirror sends beam to disc

Photodiode detects the laser beam

Bar codes

A bar code is a group of numbers that can be read using light reflected from a laser. Thick and thin strips make up each number.

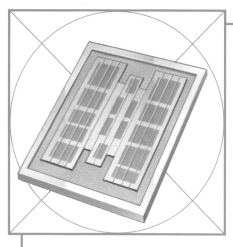

THINKING MACHINES

A computer can be "programmed" to carry out many different tasks. It can even monitor itself as it works. At the heart of a computer is an intricate system of tiny electronic circuits, packed into components called 'microchips'. Pulses of electricity travel through a microchip, carrying information which can be stored, processed, or used to make something move in action.

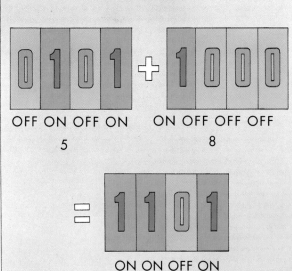

The brain

Eyes and ears take in information from the outside world

Muscles make the body move

Electric motors make precise movements

Bones provide something rigid for the muscles to pull against

Hydraulic pistons provide power

Metal framework

A computer works by representing numbers with 'on' or 'off' signals

Computer signals

A computer works in the same way as your brain, using electrical signals. Computers have only 2 kinds of signal – 'on' or 'off'. These are used to build up larger "binary" numbers. A binary number can stand for all kinds of information, from a letter in a word to a dot in a picture. Computers process information by carrying out binary calculations at great speed.

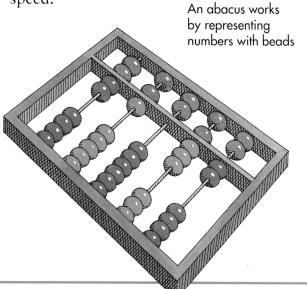

An abacus works by representing numbers with beads

0 1 0 1 + 1 0 0 0

OFF ON OFF ON   ON OFF OFF OFF

5   8

= 1 1 0 1

ON ON OFF ON

13

Robots

A robot works rather like the human body. Its muscles are electric motors or hydraulic pistons, and its brain is a computer. Robots and humans differ in a vital way: unlike a human, a robot can only follow its instructions (program).

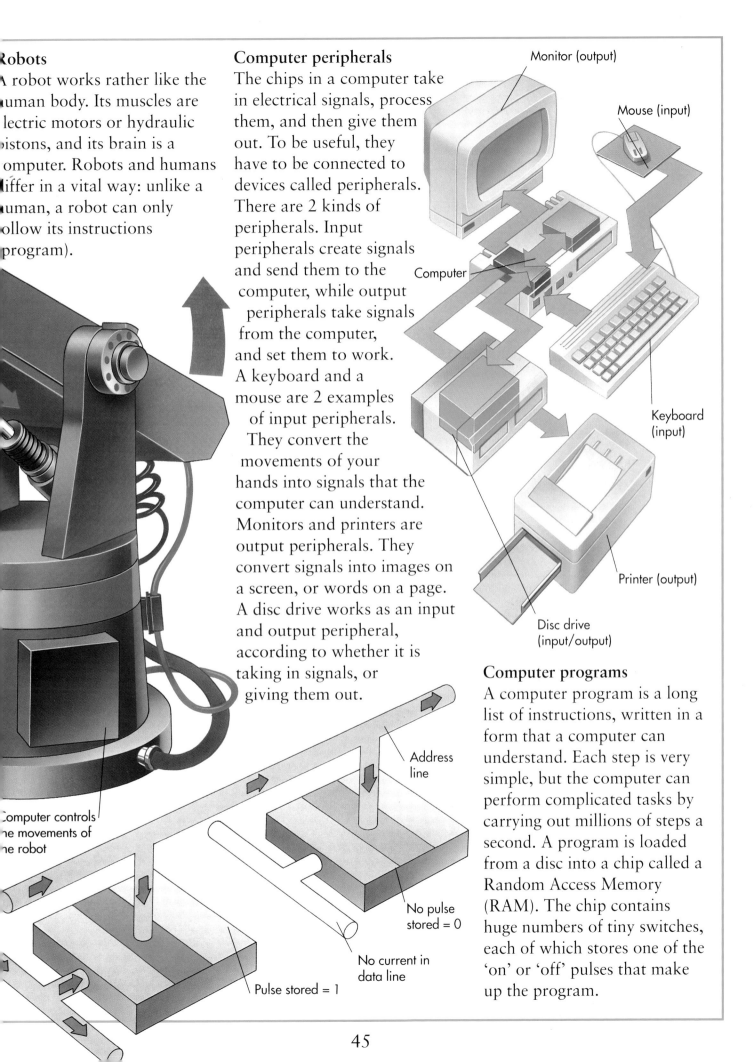

Computer controls the movements of the robot

Computer peripherals

The chips in a computer take in electrical signals, process them, and then give them out. To be useful, they have to be connected to devices called peripherals. There are 2 kinds of peripherals. Input peripherals create signals and send them to the computer, while output peripherals take signals from the computer, and set them to work. A keyboard and a mouse are 2 examples of input peripherals. They convert the movements of your hands into signals that the computer can understand. Monitors and printers are output peripherals. They convert signals into images on a screen, or words on a page. A disc drive works as an input and output peripheral, according to whether it is taking in signals, or giving them out.

Monitor (output)

Mouse (input)

Computer

Keyboard (input)

Printer (output)

Disc drive (input/output)

Address line

No pulse stored = 0

No current in data line

Pulse stored = 1

Computer programs

A computer program is a long list of instructions, written in a form that a computer can understand. Each step is very simple, but the computer can perform complicated tasks by carrying out millions of steps a second. A program is loaded from a disc into a chip called a Random Access Memory (RAM). The chip contains huge numbers of tiny switches, each of which stores one of the 'on' or 'off' pulses that make up the program.

45

INDEX